This book belongs to

UNION: Learning to Live Loved in Christ
© 2025 The Well Summit

Written by Nika Spaulding
with contributions from Jenn Jett Barrett

Designed by Jenn Jett Barrett
Photography by Laura Frazier
Published by The Well Summit

United States of America

Scripture quotations are taken from the following translations:
Christian Standard Bible® (CSB®)
Copyright © 2017 by Holman Bible Publishers. Used by permission.
The Message® (MSG®)
Copyright © 1993, 2002, 2018 by Eugene H. Peterson. Used by permission.
English Standard Version® (ESV®)
Copyright © 2001 by Crossway, a publishing ministry of Good News Publishers. Used by permission.
All rights reserved.

This study is an invitation into spiritual formation, discipleship and personal reflection. Engage at your own pace, and seek additional support when needed. The practices offered here are meant to guide and invite, not replace professional care.

ISBN:979-8-9944485-0-2

UNION

LEARNING TO LIVE LOVED IN CHRIST

Be expectant without expectations

OUR PRAYER FOR
YOU IS THAT YOU
WILL EXPERIENCE
THE GRACE OF
THE LORD JESUS
CHRIST, AND THE
LOVE OF GOD,
AND THE
FELLOWSHIP OF
THE HOLY SPIRIT

2 CORINTHIANS 13:14

Hello Beloved Sojourner,

At The Well Summit, we believe we fulfill our mission when individuals are living in:

- Union with Jesus
- Unity with Others
- Unleashed to bring the Kingdom near.

To that end, this 6-week guide invites you all to pause, reflect, and hear from God. We want to help you develop new ways of thinking and rhythms that will lead to greater **union with Jesus.**

We encourage you to use this guide as a companion, a hand to hold on a journey to connection. Maybe even consider gathering a group of friends and going through this guide together. However you go, go at a pace that allows the cultivation of rest and revelation from God.

Each week includes:

- Lectio Divina to help you linger in Scripture,
- Practices to help you recognize and name what you think, feel, and believe about God and yourself,
- Short devotional to stir reflect on,
- And, weekly practice to guide you to greater union.

Our prayer for you is that you will experience the **grace** of the Lord Jesus Christ, and the **love** of God, and the **fellowship** of the Holy Spirit (2 Cor 13:14).

~The Well Summit Team

ELEMENTS OF THIS STUDY

EACH SESSION INCLUDES A RHYTHM OF

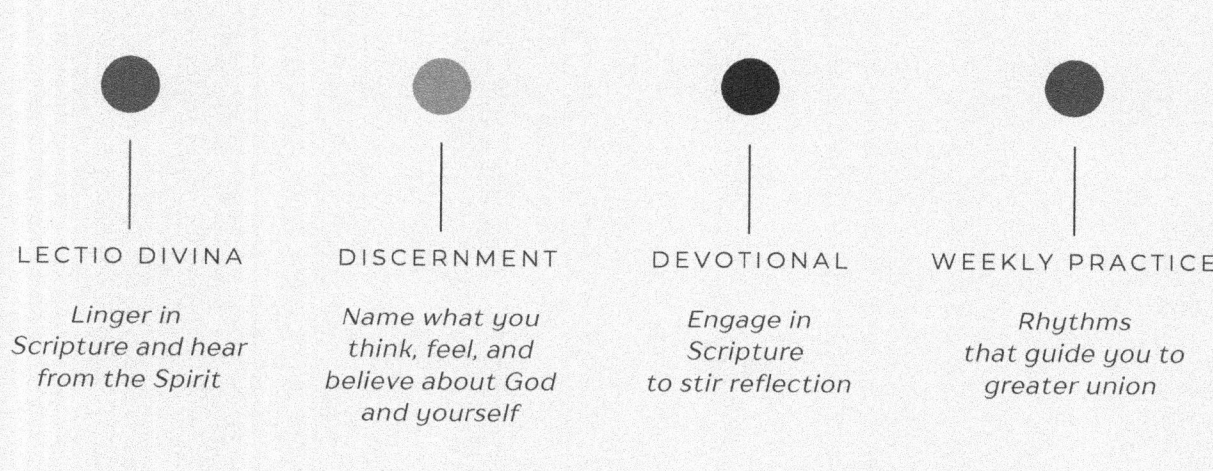

LECTIO DIVINA

*Linger in
Scripture and hear
from the Spirit*

DISCERNMENT

*Name what you
think, feel, and
believe about God
and yourself*

DEVOTIONAL

*Engage in
Scripture
to stir reflection*

WEEKLY PRACTICE

*Rhythms
that guide you to
greater union*

MOVE THROUGH AT YOUR OWN PACE

LECTIO

Each week, you'll be guided to pay attention to your inner world —your thoughts, emotions, beliefs, and longings. These simple practices help you notice what's true, what's distorted, and where God may be gently inviting you into deeper honesty, healing, and trust.

DISCERNMENT

Lectio Divina is a slow, prayerful way of reading the Bible that creates space to listen for God's voice. Instead of rushing through the passage, you'll linger—allowing a word, phrase, or invitation from the Holy Spirit to rise to the surface.

DEVOTIONAL

A brief devotional will root you in Scripture and provide a spark for reflection. These teachings are intentionally simple and open-handed, offering a starting point for conversation with the Lord rather than a list of answers.

WEEKLY PRACTICE

Every week includes a tangible, doable practice that helps you live what you're learning. These small steps—whether silence, examen, presence, or a simple act of obedience—cultivate rhythms that draw you into deeper union with Christ in your daily life.

HOW TO ENGAGE A LECTIO

ASK THE LORD TO QUIET YOUR MIND AND SOUL.
GROUND YOUR BODY AND TAKE A FEW DEEP BREATHS.
UNCLENCH YOUR JAW AND PUT YOUR FEET ON THE FLOOR.

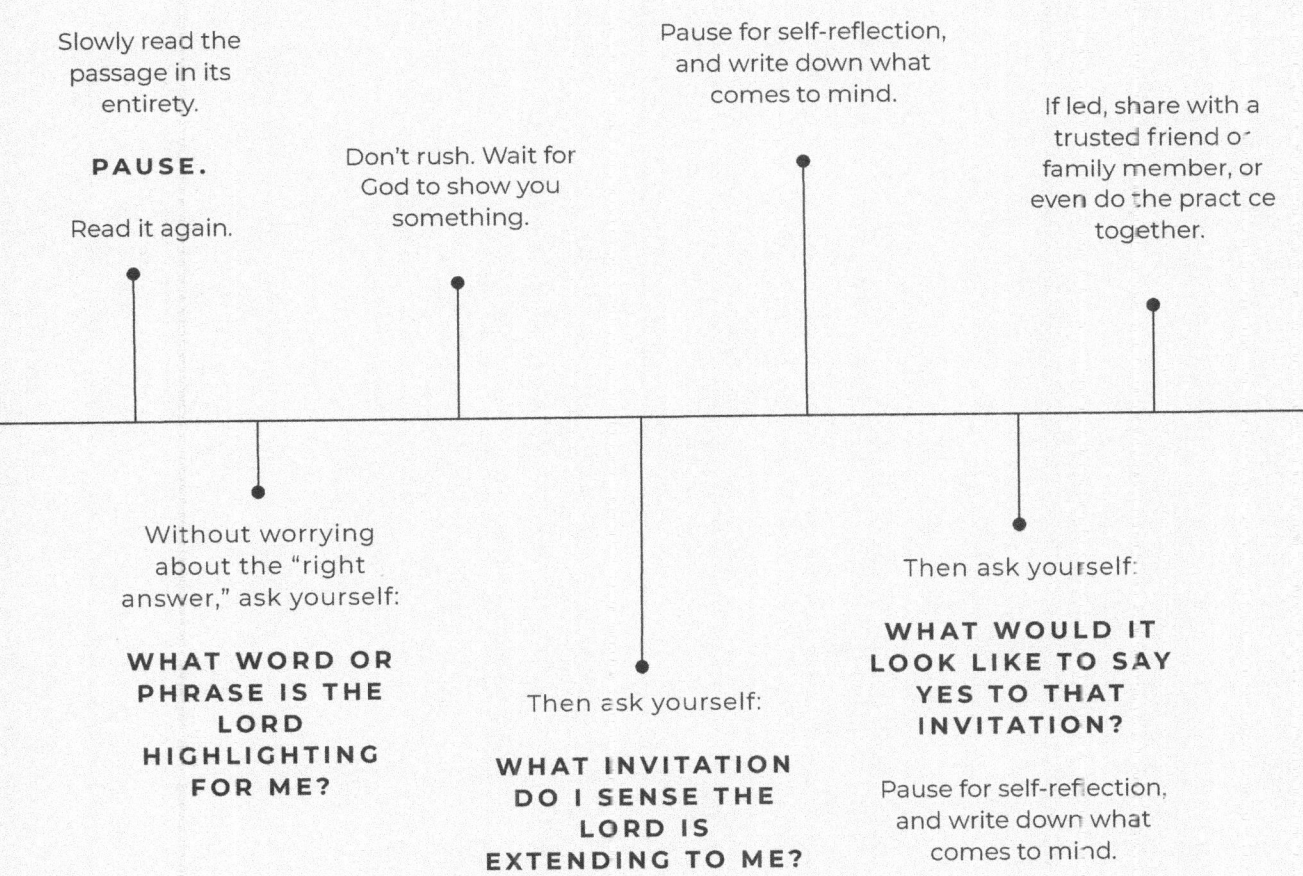

Slowly read the passage in its entirety.

PAUSE.

Read it again.

Don't rush. Wait for God to show you something.

Pause for self-reflection, and write down what comes to mind.

If led, share with a trusted friend or family member, or even do the practice together.

Without worrying about the "right answer," ask yourself:

WHAT WORD OR PHRASE IS THE LORD HIGHLIGHTING FOR ME?

Then ask yourself:

WHAT INVITATION DO I SENSE THE LORD IS EXTENDING TO ME?

Then ask yourself:

WHAT WOULD IT LOOK LIKE TO SAY YES TO THAT INVITATION?

Pause for self-reflection, and write down what comes to mind.

"GOD'S WORD GIVES LANGUAGE FOR THE HOLY SPIRIT TO SPEAK."

LECTIO DIVINA

Make your home in me

"Live in me. Make your home in me just as I do in you. In the same way that a branch can't bear grapes by itself but only by being joined to the vine, you can't bear fruit unless you are joined with me.

"I am the Vine, you are the branches. When you're joined with me and I with you, the relationship is intimate and organic, the harvest is sure to be abundant. Separated, you can't produce a thing. Anyone who separates from me is deadwood, gathered up and thrown on the bonfire. But if you make yourselves at home with me and my words are at home in you, you can be sure that whatever you ask will be listened to and acted upon. This is how my Father shows who he is—when you produce grapes, when you mature as my disciples.

"I've loved you the way my Father has loved me. Make yourselves at home in my love. If you keep my commands, you'll remain intimately at home in my love. That's what I've done—kept my Father's commands and made myself at home in his love.

"I've told you these things for a purpose: that my joy might be your joy, and your joy wholly mature."

JOHN 15:4-11
THE MESSAGE

READ THE PASSAGE TWICE

WHAT WORD OR PHRASE IS THE LORD HIGHLIGHTING FOR ME?

PAUSE

WHAT INVITATION DO I SENSE THE LORD IS EXTENDING TO ME?

PAUSE

WHAT WOULD IT LOOK LIKE TO SAY "YES" TO THAT INVITATION?

How to Engage a Lectio Divina: page 9

Take a moment and ask yourself, what comes to mind when I think of "union with Jesus"? What words, phrases, and images pop into your head?

WHAT IS UNION WITH JESUS?

What is your earliest understanding of salvation? How has your understanding of salvation changed over time? What about your first understanding of union with Jesus? How has that changed over time?

The Bible presents salvation in a myriad of ways: justification, adoption, redemption, etc. While some ways of thinking about salvation are immediate and transactional, others are ongoing and relational. *All* of these ways are important to understanding just how great a gift salvation is.

Both the image of a gavel slamming down while we're declared innocent—justification—and an embrace of a loving father who brings us into his family—adoption—help us understand better our relationship to God.

Union with Jesus is one of the ways the New Testament writers understood what takes place at the moment of conversion *and* throughout the life of the believer. **It happens to be both immediate *and* ongoing in nature.**

The gospel doesn't just secure our eternity—it shapes and transforms us every single day.

In his letter to the Romans, Paul argues that all of humanity was *in* Adam—united to our first father. This also meant all who were *in* Adam suffered under the corruption and frailty from the effects of the fall in Genesis 3.

But for those who welcome the Gospel, we are now *in* Christ, and united to the healing and restoration the resurrection brings. We transfer our union from Adam into Christ, and that transfer saves us completely.

Pause for a moment and let that sink in. We are now *in* Christ, and united to the healing and restoration the resurrection brings. We transfer our union from Adam into Christ, and that transfer saves us completely.

But union with Jesus also does more than save; it opens us up to an infinitely deep well of spiritual nourishment, power, and healing. Immediate *and* ongoing.

REFLECT ——

How do these verses help you understand the *immediate* nature of union with Christ?:

- Romans 6:5-6
- Colossians 3:3

How do these verses help you understand the *ongoing* nature of union with Christ?:

- John 15:4-5
- Colossians 2:6-7

Union continues through the life-long practices, rhythms, and habits that help us to dwell with God in Christ.

This means salvation is the doorway to union with Jesus—the entrance we must all pass through at some point when we say yes to the unbelievable invitation to enter into the life of God in Christ. But once you cross that threshold, **union has only just begun**. It continues throughout the life-long practices, rhythms, and habits that help us to dwell *with* God in Christ.

In union, we learn to abide in Christ daily, drawing our life, strength, and identity from Him. This results in Spirit-empowered obedience, love of others, and a reshaping of our views of God, others, and ourselves.

RE-SHAPING OUR UNDERSTANDING OF UNION

Take a moment to meditate on the idea of *union in Christ.* What words, phrases, and images help you to make sense of this big idea?

What would a life completely united to Christ look like? How would it feel? How would others experience you if you were completely united to Jesus?

What questions do you have about union with Christ?

PRAY

Take some time to pray, ask the Lord to show you ways you can grow in your union in Christ. Do not rush the prayer; wait on God to show you.

Then close your prayer with:

Lord, help me to long for greater intimacy with you. Teach me what union with you looks like. Help me to find my rest at home united to you.

Inhale: *I am in you.*
Exhale: *Help me to remain.*

DEVOTIONAL

JOHN 15:4-11 MSG

"Live in me. Make your home in me just as I do in you. In the same way that a branch can't bear grapes by itself but only by being joined to the vine, you can't bear fruit unless you are joined with me.

I am the Vine, you are the branches. When you're joined with me and I with you, the relation intimate and organic, the harvest is sure to be abundant. Separated, you can't produce a thing. Anyone who separates from me is deadwood, gathered up and thrown on the bonfire. But if you make yourselves at home with me and my words are at home in you, you can be sure that whatever you ask will be listened to and acted upon. This is how my Father shows who he is—when you produce grapes, when you mature as my disciples.

I've loved you the way my Father has loved me. Make yourselves at home in my love. If you keep my commands, you'll remain intimately at home in my love. That's what I've done—kept my Father's commands and made myself at home in his love.

I've told you these things for a purpose: that my joy might be your joy, and your joy wholly mature."

Jesus loves illustrations from the natural world—trees, mountains, seeds. It is no surprise then that he paints a beautiful picture of union to him with a vivid, garden image: a branch connected to a vine.

Notice the branch no longer has to grit its teeth or strain to produce fruit; it must simply stay connected to its life source and watch the fruit mature as life flows through it. This is the same way for the life of the believer. Instead of manufacturing holiness or striving for joy and peace on our own strength, Jesus invites us to borrow his strength.

We are invited to remain—abide—in Christ, receiving Jesus' life as our own.

This makes union with Jesus both a gift and a practice. We are united to Jesus by the Spirit, and now he invites us to stay connected through spiritual practices, obedience, surrender, and resting in his love.

When we remain, then the fruit—love, joy, peace, patience, etc—flows from the steady flow of his life in us, not from frantic, frenetic effort.

If you want greater peace, wholeness, joy, and love, according to Jesus, it's not about doing more but about dwelling deeper.

REFLECTION QUESTIONS

WHAT DOES "REMAINING IN CHRIST" LOOK LIKE IN MY DAILY RHYTHMS OF WORK,
REST, AND RELATIONSHIPS?

WHERE AM I TRYING TO PRODUCE FRUIT APART FROM JESUS? WHERE AM
I LEARNING TO REST IN HIM?

WHERE MIGHT JESUS BE INVITING ME TO SLOW DOWN AND SIMPLY REMAIN IN HIS
LOVE TODAY?

RHYTHMS THAT CULTIVATE UNION

WHAT IS JESUS INVITING ME TO CULTIVATE?

WORK	REST	RELATIONSHIPS

WHAT IS JESUS INVITING ME TO REMOVE?

WORK	REST	RELATIONSHIPS

WRITE A PRAYER OF INTENTION FOR HOW YOU WANT TO DRAW NEAR TO JESUS MORE INTENTIONALLY IN THIS NEXT SEASON

As a way of orienting ourselves to Jesus each morning and to practice our union in Christ, we encourage you to start your day this way:

Take a moment to settle your mind and inhale and exhale deeply.

Pray the following: *Jesus, I give you my thoughts, my hands, my steps, my desires, and my worries.*

Then, spend some time imagining each one. Then imagine handing each one over to God – the activities and worries of your day and trusting him to help you handle them.

Inhale: *Christ lives in me.*
Exhale: *I dwell in him.*

MY HANDS

MY STEPS

MY DESIRES

LECTIO DIVINA

God met me more than halfway

I bless God every chance I get; my lungs expand with his praise.

I live and breathe God; if things aren't going well, hear this and be happy:

Join me in spreading the news; together let's get the word out.

God met me more than halfway, he freed me from my anxious fears.

Look at him; give him your warmest smile. Never hide your feelings from him.

When I was desperate, I called out, and God got me out of a tight spot.

God's angel sets up a circle of protection around us while we pray.

Open your mouth and taste, open your eyes and see—how good God is.

Blessed are you who run to him.

Worship God if you want the best; worship opens doors to all his goodness.

Young lions on the prowl get hungry, but God-seekers are full of God.

Come, children, listen closely; I'll give you a lesson in God worship.

Who out there has a lust for life? Can't wait each day to come upon beauty?

Guard your tongue from profanity, and no more lying through your teeth. Turn your back on sin; do something good.

Embrace peace—don't let it get away!

God keeps an eye on his friends, his ears pick up every moan and groan.

God won't put up with rebels; he'll cull them from the pack.

Is anyone crying for help? God is listening, ready to rescue you.

If your heart is broken, you'll find God right there; if you're kicked in the gut, he'll help you catch your breath.

Disciples so often get into trouble; still, God is there every time.

He's your bodyguard, shielding every bone; not even a finger gets broken.

The wicked commit slow suicide; they waste their lives hating the good.

God pays for each slave's freedom; no one who runs to him loses out.

PSALM 34
THE MESSAGE

READ THE PASSAGE TWICE

WHAT WORD OR PHRASE IS THE LORD HIGHLIGHTING FOR ME?

PAUSE

WHAT INVITATION DO I SENSE THE LORD IS EXTENDING TO ME?

PAUSE

WHAT WOULD IT LOOK LIKE TO SAY "YES" TO THAT INVITATION?

IMAGINE

Take a moment and imagine yourself sitting in a chair facing another, empty chair. Settle yourself, relax, take some deep breaths.

Now, imagine God comes and sits in the chair in front of you.

What is going on in your body?

How does it feel to sit before God?

What do you think God thinks of you?

What does God feel toward you?

In his book The Knowledge of the Holy AW Tozer states, "**What comes into our minds when we think about God is the most important thing about us.**"

Tozer makes this claim because our concept of God shapes our entire lives. He realized what so many throughout history also concludec— theology is more than an abstract exercise of the mind; it drives our ground-level decisions.

If we perceive God as distant, harsh, or small, we will live in a state of detachment from God, struggling to find rest and peace. But if we know and experience God as loving, good, and near, then our lives will reflect that with greater unity in Christ, resulting in peace, joy, and love.

"What comes into our minds when we think about God is the most important thing about us."

AW TOZER

PRAYERFULLY MEDITATE ON THE FOLLOWING QUESTIONS

WHAT HAS INFLUENCED AND SHAPED YOUR VIEW OF GOD?

WHAT WERE HELPFUL INFLUENCES? HARMFUL?

CAN YOU THINK OF A MOMENT WHEN YOU FELT ESPECIALLY CLOSE TO AND LOVED BY GOD?

WHAT DID IT FEEL LIKE?

PRAYERFULLY MEDITATE ON THE FOLLOWING QUESTIONS

WHEN YOU THINK OF THE SCRIPTURES, WHAT PASSAGES, METAPHORS, IMAGES, OR MOMENTS CAN YOU MEDITATE UPON THAT WILL HELP YOU BETTER FORM YOUR IMAGE OF GOD?

WHEN YOU SIT DOWN TO PRAY TO GOD, WHAT ARE YOUR FIRST THOUGHTS OR FEELINGS?

Take a moment and write down 5 words that describe God and how you want to experience him. Then ask God to help you experience those words this week.

Inhale: *God, you are love.*
Exhale: *You love me.*

DEVOTIONAL

EXODUS 34:4-7 CSB

"Moses cut two stone tablets like the first ones. He got up early in the morning, and taking the two stone tablets in his hand, he climbed Mount Sinai, just as the Lord had commanded him.

The Lord came down in a cloud, stood with him there, and proclaimed his name, "the Lord." The Lord passed in front of him and proclaimed:

"The Lord—the Lord is a compassionate and gracious God, slow to anger and abounding in faithful love and truth, maintaining faithful love to a thousand generations, forgiving iniquity, rebellion, and sin. But he will not leave the guilty unpunished, bringing the consequences of the fathers' iniquity on the children and grandchildren to the third and fourth generation.""

These are perhaps some of the most famous and repeated words in the Bible when trying to describe God's character. They come at a crucial moment in Israel's history. The people, by worshipping the golden calf, broke their covenant with God.

Now their future hangs in the balance as Moses begs God to show them mercy. Would God abandon them? Would His presence still go with them?

Unwilling to continue the journey to the Promised Land without God, Moses begged for assurance that God would still be with his people. In response, God revealed not only His presence but His very character. As He passed before Moses, God gave a self-declaration: This is who I am. It is one of the clearest places in the Bible where God describes Himself.

WHO IS GOD?

God is compassionate and gracious. God's disposition is to move toward his people in mercy, even and perhaps especially, when they fail.

God is slow to anger. God's patience is greater than our rebellion. He is not a God that flies off the handle, but is measured and long-suffering.

God abounds in love and faithfulness. His covenant love (hesed) sticks to us no matter what. His love does not come and go with our performance but remains through every peak and valley.

God forgives deeply. Sin, rebellion, evil—all of humanity's failures—can be forgiven through Jesus.

God is also just. His goodness means He does not wink at evil. God is gracious, but he is also good, which means he will act on behalf of the oppressed.

DO YOU BELIEVE GOD IS WHO HE SAYS HE IS?

If this is who God is, why do we avoid God?

We often do not dwell *with* God because we imagine God wants nothing to do with us. We think that instead of wanting us to draw near, God is angry, disappointed, or distant from us.

This passage in Exodus shows that even in our biggest moments of failure, God's character does not change ... which means his desire to be near us stays the same as well.

God wants to draw near to you, and wants you to draw near to God.

REFLECTION QUESTIONS

Which character(s) of God are easiest for you to know and experience? Hardest? Why do you suppose that is?

How have you "blown it" like the Israelites? Can you imagine God saying the same things to you today?

If you had to reword this self-declaration of God with language you use regularly—metaphors, examples, images—how would you describe God's character?

How does this story in the Scriptures inform your understanding of *union* with Christ?

Put yourself in the shoes of the Israelites. God has just rescued you from Egypt and invited you to covenant with him as partners in a grand mission. Then you utterly fail. Completely blow it. And God responds with this merciful declaration. How might that have felt?

IMAGINE

Take a moment during a slow part of your day to carve out time for this exercise.

Imagine yourself sitting in a chair facing another empty chair. Settle yourself, relax, take some deep breaths.

Now, imagine God comes and sits in the chair in front of you and looks at you with love and delight.

Imagine God tells you that you are his image bearer— worthy of dignity.

Imagine God tells you that he wants to be *with* you forever, so he made a way for you to be united by the finished work of the Son and the indwelling of the Spirit.

Imagine God tells you that he forgives your sins and does not want anything to come between you.

Now, imagine what it would be like to dwell daily with a God of love, compassion, mercy, and justice.

Pray: *God, help me to see you as you really are. As you show yourself to be. Help me remove the areas where I have wrongly formed you in my imagination and replace them with the truth. Teach me to know you and to walk with you all the days of my life.*

Inhale: *God's character never changes.*
Exhale: *God wants me to draw near.*

LECTIO DIVINA

You were saved by grace

Lord, you have searched me and known me.

You know when I sit down and when I stand up; you understand my thoughts from far away.

You observe my travels and my rest; you are aware of all my ways.

Before a word is on my tongue, you know all about it, Lord.

You have encircled me; you have placed your hand on me.

This wondrous knowledge is beyond me. It is lofty; I am unable to reach it.

Where can I go to escape your Spirit?
Where can I flee from your presence?

If I go up to heaven, you are there;
if I make my bed in Sheol, you are there.

If I fly on the wings of the dawn and settle down on the western horizon, even there your hand will lead me; your right hand will hold on to me.

If I say, "Surely the darkness will hide me, and the light around me will be night"—

even the darkness is not dark to you.
The night shines like the day;
darkness and light are alike to you.

For it was you who created my inward parts; you knit me together in my mother's womb.

I will praise you because I have been remarkably and wondrously made. Your works are wondrous, and I know this very well.

My bones were not hidden from you when I was made in secret, when I was formed in the depths of the earth.

Your eyes saw me when I was formless; all my days were written in your book and planned before a single one of them began.

God, how precious your thoughts are to me; how vast their sum is!

If I counted them, they would outnumber the grains of sand; when I wake up, I am still with you.

God, if only you would kill the wicked—you bloodthirsty men, stay away from me—who invoke you deceitfully.

Your enemies swear by you falsely.

Lord, don't I hate those who hate you, and detest those who rebel against you?

I hate them with extreme hatred; I consider them my enemies.

Search me, God, and know my heart; test me and know my concerns.

See if there is any offensive way in me; lead me in the everlasting way.

PSALM 139
CSB

The path toward greater union with Christ is not paved through neutral territory. It weaves through enemy territory with obstacles and disorientation along the way.

The enemy's go-to weapons—**lies, fears, shame, sin, distractions, and unprocessed grief**—act like lassos tightening around us and yanking us away from the Lord. This session provides an opportunity to take inventory about what currently entangles you, so that you can move forward toward healing.

In the same way, these **six questions** are an invitation from God to examine your inner world. The space where Jesus longs to dwell. It's a chance to bring your thoughts and feelings to Him, trusting Him to guide you toward healing and alignment with His truth. And with every invitation He offers, He's taking you somewhere worth going.

BEST PRACTICES

Take time to read each question and be aware of the ones the Spirit is inviting you to answer.

You may find yourself answering just one, or two, or all of them.

Be patient and take the time that you need. You don't have to finish this whole practice in one sitting or at all.

The aim of the exercise is to search, discern, and turn to God for healing.

David's prayer in Psalm 139:23-24

"Search me, O God, and know my heart; test me and know my anxious thoughts,"

invites God to look deeply and honestly into his thoughts and emotions and lead him toward truth and peace.

SIX CURIOUS QUESTIONS

1 What lie(s) are you believing about yourself, others, or God?

Take every thought captive to make it obedient to Christ. - **2 CORINTHIANS 10:5**

Sometimes the lies we believe have been words literally spoken over us that we made agreements with. Other times it is the *father of lies* who deliberately deceives us into believing things about ourselves, others, and God that are not true. We have to know truth to discern what is the voice of the enemy and what is the voice of God.

VOICE OF THE ENEMY

- Brings condemnation and shame, often pointing out failures without offering hope.
- *You're not enough. God could never forgive you.*
- Distorts God's character, making Him seem distant, harsh, or uncaring.
- *God doesn't love you. He's forgotten you.*
- Causes fear, confusion, or discouragement.
- Twists Scripture to manipulate or deceive.

VOICE OF GOD

- Brings conviction without condemnation. God's correction leads to repentance and growth.
- Aligns with Scripture. God's voice will never contradict His Word.
- Produces peace, even in difficult circumstances.
- Encourages and builds you up, reminding you of your identity in Christ.
- *You are my beloved child. You belong. You are chosen. You are forgiven.*

ASK THE LORD TO HELP YOU
DISCERN TRUTH FROM LIES.
HE WILL DO IT.

2 What fear is consuming you?

So do not fear, for I am with you; do not be dismayed, for I am your God. I will strengthen you and help you; I will uphold you with my righteous right hand.
- ISAIAH 41:10

Even if there is a very real danger, fear is imagining a future without Jesus. Where did that fear come from? Where is He wanting you to trust Him?

3 What shame is destroying your sense of self?

In place of your shame, you will have a double portion; in place of disgrace, they will rejoice over their share. So they will possess double in their land, and eternal joy will be theirs. - ISAIAH 61:7

Shame messages tell us that we are fundamentally broken and unworthy of love and acceptance. What messages are you currently believing that bring you shame? How is the Lord inviting you to see yourself through His eyes?

4 What sin, unforgiveness, or idols are entangling you?

Therefore, confess your sins to one another and pray for one another, so that you may be healed. JAMES 5:16

God's conviction is kind. Confession leads us toward healing, not shame. What feels heavy or tangled within you, and where is Jesus inviting you to bring it into the light in a way that leads to healing?

5 What distractions are derailing you?

Be alert and of sober mind. - I PETER 5:8

———

What is competing for your time and attention? Is it social media, devices, striving, unhealthy friendships, busyness, or co-dependency? Is the Lord inviting you to abide?

6 What grief needs to be processed?

Blessed are those who mourn, for they will be comforted. - *Matthew 5:4*

———

God grieves and laments what He never intended. Genesis 6:6 says, His heart broke over the sin in the world: this in between Eden and New Heaven of broken families, broken marriages, broken relationships, broken bodies. One third of the psalms are psalms of lament.

What needs to be lamented? Where does the Lord want to meet you with comfort?

Take some time after reflecting and ask the Lord to heal whatever is hurting, restore whatever is broken, and resurrect whatever is dead. And then graciously give him time to do it.

Inhale: *I am yours.*
Exhale: *I want to be with you.*

Each question is an invitation

These questions can become a regular rhythm to
return to anytime you sense unrest, confusion, or
disorientation. It is not a one time exercise but an
ongoing rhythm that will continue to invite you into
understanding more of the fullness of God's love and
character.

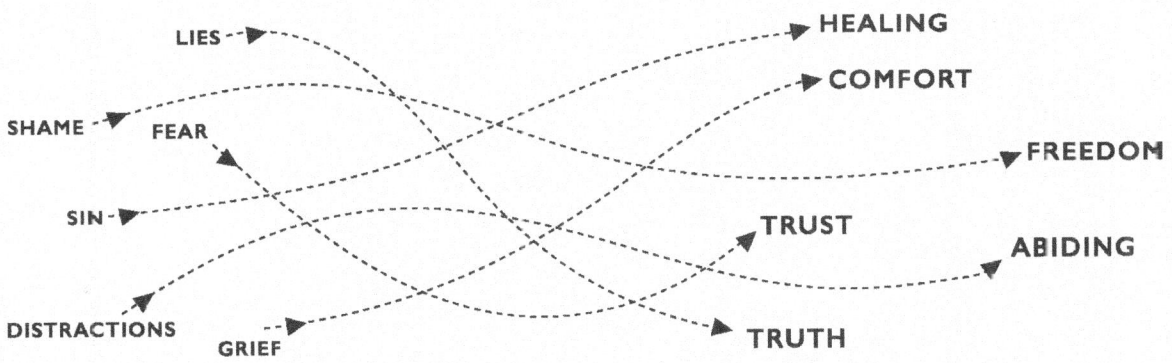

Lies - The Lord wants to lead you to Truth
Fear - The Lord wants to lead you to Trust
Shame - The Lord wants to lead you to Freedom
Confessing Sin, Idols, Unforgiveness - The Lord wants to lead you to Healing
Distractions - The Lord wants to lead you to Abide
Grief - The Lord wants to lead you to Comfort

DEVOTIONAL

EPHESIANS 2:1-10 CSB

"And you were dead in your trespasses and sins in which you previously walked according to the ways of this world, according to the ruler of the power of the air, the spirit now working in the disobedient. We too all previously lived among them in our fleshly desires, carrying out the inclinations of our flesh and thoughts, and we were by nature children under wrath as the others were also. But God, who is rich in mercy, because of his great love that he had for us, made us alive with Christ even though we were dead in trespasses. You are saved by grace! He also raised us up with him and seated us with him in the heavens in Christ Jesus, so that in the coming ages he might display the immeasurable riches of his grace through his kindness to us in Christ Jesus. For you are saved by grace through faith, and this is not from yourselves; it is God's gift—not from works, so that no one can boast. For we are his workmanship, created in Christ Jesus for good works, which God prepared ahead of time for us to do."

Paul paints two stark pictures in this passage. The first is our life apart from Christ: *"dead in trespasses and sins, following the course of this world, following the prince of the power of the air... carrying out the desires of the flesh"* (vv. 1–3).

Here we see the enemy's schemes at work—twisting the **world's** patterns, stirring up **fleshly** desires, and keeping us captive under the **enemy's** schemes. It's an unholy trinity of sorts—world, flesh, enemy.

Notice, too, that Paul says we are not just folks who made mistakes. We're prisoners of war that has left us **dead**. Powerless. Enslaved. Hopeless.

But then come two of the most beautiful words in Scripture:

BUT GOD.

HOLY TRINITY

GOD
THE
FATHER

GOD
THE
SON

GOD
THE
HOLY SPIRIT

unholy trinity

world

flesh

enemy

Notice the shift—from slavery to union. From death to resurrection life. From shame to grace. Because of the Father's love, the Son's obedience, and the Spirit's enlivening, we not only are alive again, but we have the privilege of being united with Christ as he currently sits in the heavenly realm.

Take a moment and really consider this ... the greatest rags to riches story ever told is that of humanity in Christ.

With a flourish of his pen, Paul shows how being *united to Jesus* **changes everything:**

- We are raised up with Him.
- We are seated with Him in the heavenly places.
- We are living testimonies of His immeasurable grace.
- We are his instruments to bring peace to the world.
- We are given spiritual gifts to help build up the church and the world.

The enemy enslaves with lies. Christ frees with love. The enemy's schemes end in wrath. Christ's riches end in eternal life.

The path to union with Christ might go through enemy territory, but we have a faithful shepherd who leads us to greener pastures. When you are struggling to abide with Christ, let Ephesians remind you that there's an enemy that makes it hard. Then, use that as motivation to turn to Christ and receive the unbelievable gifts God bestows upon us.

> In the face of the enemy's schemes, God overwhelms us with His riches: "God, being rich in mercy, because of the great love with which he loved us, even when we were dead... made us alive together with Christ" (vv. 4–5).

REFLECTION QUESTIONS

HOW DO YOU SEE THE SCHEMES OF EVIL IN THE WORLD, YOUR OWN FLESH, AND THE
ENEMY THAT SEEKS TO STEAL, KILL, AND DESTROY YOU?

HOW DOES IT MAKE YOU FEEL TO KNOW THAT THERE IS AN ENEMY THAT WANTS TO
PULL YOU AWAY FROM UNION WITH CHRIST?

HOW WOULD YOU PUT INTO YOUR OWN WORDS THE SCHEMES OF EVIL COMPARED TO
THE GIFTS OF GOD?

Inhale: *God offers me gifts.*
Exhale: *I receive these gifts.*

EPHESIANS 6:10-18 NLT

"A final word: Be strong in the Lord and in his mighty power. Put on all of God's armor so that you will be able to stand firm against all strategies of the devil. For we are not fighting against flesh-and-blood enemies, but against evil rulers and authorities of the unseen world, against mighty powers in this dark world, and against evil spirits in the heavenly places.

Therefore, put on every piece of God's armor so you will be able to resist the enemy in the time of evil. Then after the battle you will still be standing firm. Stand your ground, putting on the belt of truth and the body armor of God's righteousness. For shoes, put on the peace that comes from the Good News so that you will be fully prepared. In addition to all of these, hold up the shield of faith to stop the fiery arrows of the devil. Put on salvation as your helmet, and take the sword of the Spirit, which is the word of God.

Pray in the Spirit at all times and on every occasion. Stay alert and be persistent in your prayers for all believers everywhere."

PRAY

While Paul is sober-minded about the schemes of the enemy and the very real danger it poses to believers, he also knows we are not defenseless. At the end of Ephesians, Paul encourages believers to put on the full armor of God to stand firm.

This week, we invite you to mentally rehearse putting on the full armor and asking God to help you remain in his strength.

PUTTING ON THE FULL ARMOR

Find a quiet space. Take a few deep breaths. As you breathe in, remind yourself that you are in Christ, and as you breathe out, let go of distractions.

Pray,
"Lord, help me to stand firm in your strength."

Belt of Truth

Imagine fastening a strong, wide belt around your waist. This belt represents God's truth holding everything together.

Pray: *"Lord, fasten Your truth around me. Let me reject lies and walk in integrity."*

Reflect: Where might the enemy be tempting me to believe lies? How does God's Word correct them?

Breastplate of Righteousness

Picture a solid chest plate being placed over your heart. It guards your core—your identity in Christ.

Pray: *"Father, protect my heart. Help me trust in the righteousness of Christ, not my own performance."*

Reflect: What areas of guilt or shame need to be covered by Christ's righteousness today?

Peaceful Kicks

Visualize lacing up sturdy shoes, giving you firm footing and readiness to move forward in God's peace.

Pray: *"Lord, help me stand on the peace You have given me, and guide my steps to bring Your peace to others."*

Reflect: Where can I carry God's peace today?

Shield of Faith

Imagine lifting up a large, protective shield in front of you. It catches fiery arrows of doubt, fear, or temptation and anything else the enemy sends your way.

Pray: *"Lord, strengthen my faith to trust You when I face attack."*

Reflect: What fiery darts am I facing right now—fear, discouragement, temptation?

Helmet of Salvation

Place a helmet on your head. It guards your mind with the assurance that you belong to Christ.

Pray: *"Lord, protect my thoughts. Remind me daily that I am saved by grace."*

Reflect: What anxious or negative thoughts need to be replaced with the hope of salvation?

Sword of the Spirit

Picture holding a sharp, double-edged sword—God's Word.

Pray: *"Lord, help me wield your Word with wisdom and courage."*

Reflect: Which Scripture can I carry with me today as a weapon against lies and discouragement?

IMAGINE

Finally, imagine being fully suited.
Stand tall. You are not defenseless—
you are strong in Christ.

Pray: *"Lord, help me to stay alert
and to pray for myself and others,
that we may stand firm against the
enemy."*

Inhale: *God, you are my defense.*
Exhale: *I live by your strength.*

LECTIO DIVINA

As you are in me and I am in you

"I pray not only for these, but also for those who believe in me through their word. May they all be one, as you, Father, are in me and I am in you. May they also be[e] in us, so that the world may believe you sent me. I have given them the glory you have given me, so that they may be one as we are one. I am in them and you are in me, so that they may be made completely one, that the world may know you have sent me and have loved them as you have loved me.

Father, I want those you have given me to be with me where I am, so that they will see my glory, which you have given me because you loved me before the world's foundation. Righteous Father, the world has not known you. However, I have known you, and they have known that you sent me. I made your name known to them and will continue to make it known, so that the love you have loved me with may be in them and I may be in them."

JOHN 17:20-26
CSB

READ THE PASSAGE TWICE

WHAT WORD OR PHRASE IS THE LORD HIGHLIGHTING FOR ME?

PAUSE

WHAT INVITATION DO I SENSE THE LORD IS EXTENDING TO ME?

PAUSE

WHAT WOULD IT LOOK LIKE TO SAY "YES" TO THAT INVITATION?

From the very beginning, God's desire has been to be *with* His people. In the Garden of Eden, Adam and Eve experienced the pure joy of walking with God in the cool of the day (Gen. 3:8). That picture of unhindered fellowship—no shame, no separation, no sin—shows us God's original intention for humanity: peaceful union with the Trinity.

Just imagine walking through cool grass, hearing the woosh of the Pishon River nearby. You're chewing on a freshly plucked mango and chatting with God. If you long for that, know that God wants that too.

THEN, REBELLION SHATTERED THAT CLOSENESS, BUT GOD'S HEART NEVER CHANGED.

Throughout the story of Scripture, we see God making a way back. He dwelt among His people in the tabernacle and later in the temple. He revealed His glory, offered a means to draw near through the sacrifices, and guided Israel by His presence. Then, in the fullness of time, Jesus came—Immanuel, *God with us*—bringing God's presence to humanity in the form of humanity. And when Jesus ascended, He poured out His Spirit so that God Himself might dwell *within* His people—it can't get any closer than that.

And, notice all three members of the Trinity at work in bringing us home—the Father authors our salvation, Jesus accomplishes it, and the Spirit applies it. All co-conspirators in the mission to bring us back to them.

> "Behold, the dwelling place of God is with man. He will dwell with them, and they will be his people, and God himself will be with them as their God."
>
> Revelation 21:3

SOMEDAY THE STORY WILL END WHERE IT BEGAN: IN PERFECT UNION.

Revelation 21:3 declares, *"Behold, the dwelling place of God is with man. He will dwell with them, and they will be his people, and God himself will be with them as their God."* Every page of Scripture in between Eden and eternity tells of God's relentless pursuit to make this union possible.

This is a true and trustworthy statement: God wants to be with his people. So, why don't we believe it?

77%

A study done by Baylor University titled "American Piety in the 21st Century," which surveyed over 1700 respondents, revealed that American Christianity has a substantially negative view of God. **According to this survey, 77% of people, or three out of every four people, believe God is angry, distant, or critical, or they reject God altogether.** Which means only 23% of people believe God to be active in our lives and benevolent or *for us.*

If all of Scripture declares a good God wants to be near his people, but 77% of us flat out reject this reality, how do we begin to shape our perception of God toward the reality of God revealed in his Word and actions?

While there is no simple fix, there are steps to take in the right direction. Perhaps the first step is to say yes to God's invitation—and saying yes requires we remember the ways God invites.

NATHAN WAGNON, "IT'S AS SIMPLE AS A, B, C," EDEN PROJECT, FEBRUARY 15, 2024, HTTPS://WWW.THEEDENPROJECT.COM/RESOURCES/ARTICLES/REFORM-CHANNEL/ARTICLES/GOD-THE-BRAIN-ARTICLES/ITS-AS-SIMPLE-AS-A-B-C-2/.

REMEMBERING GOD'S INVITATION

GOD'S INVITATION TO SALVATION

How did God first make His invitation of salvation clear to you?

No one can come to Me unless the Father who sent Me draws him; and I will raise him up at the last day.
John 6:44

GOD'S INVITATION TO RELATIONSHIP

How do you sense God drawing you in for greater union?

Therefore, let us approach the throne of grace with boldness, so that we may receive mercy and find grace to help us in our time of need. **Hebrews 4:16**

GOD'S INVITATION TO BRING OUR BURDENS

What burdens are you currently carrying that God is inviting you to lay down before Him?

Come to me, all of you who are weary and burdened, and I will give you rest.
Matthew 11:28

REMEMBERING GOD'S INVITATION

GOD'S INVITATION TO USE OUR SPIRITUAL GIFTS

How has God uniquely gifted you to serve His beloved bride—the body of Christ?

Just as each one has received a gift, use it to serve others, as good stewards of the varied grace of God. **1 Peter 4:10**

GOD'S INVITATION TO REST

What rhythms of rest is He inviting you to embrace right now?

I will both lie down and sleep in peace, for you alone, LORD, make me live in safety. **Psalm 4:8**

GOD'S INVITATION TO PRAYER AND WORSHIP

In what ways do you sense God inviting you to deeper prayer and more wholehearted worship?

Pray constantly, give thanks in everything; for this is God's will for you in Christ Jesus. **1 Thessalonians 5:17–18**

REMEMBERING GOD'S INVITATION

GOD'S INVITATION TO ETERNAL HOPE

Where do you need to be reminded that your story is heading toward eternal union with Him?

If I go away and prepare a place for you, I will come again and take you to myself, so that where I am you may be also. **John 14:3**

Inhale: *God invites me to draw near.*
Exhale: *I will say yes.*

DEVOTIONAL

One of the great threads of the Bible is that God is not distant—He shows up. From the first pages of Scripture to the last, we find a God who comes near to His people.

For each of these moments, take a moment to reflect on the context in which God shows up. How he responds to the people, and what this reveals about union with God.

Jot down what you learn about God's desire for union in each of these moments:

God shows up after sin
Genesis 3

God shows up when the enemy bears down
Exodus 14

God shows up to guide
Numbers 14

God shows up for battle
Joshua 6

God shows up in the midst of His people
1 Kings 8

God shows up in exile
Ezekiel 1

God shows up in person
John 1

God shows up in Spirit
Acts 2

God shows up to put an end to evil forever
Revelation 18-19

THE GOD WHO SHOWS UP IS THE SAME YESTERDAY, TODAY, AND FOREVER. HE HAS NOT CHANGED. HE DELIGHTS TO BE WITH HIS PEOPLE. HE DELIGHTS TO BE WITH YOU.

Inhale: *God delights in me.*
Exhale: *I will rest in his delight.*

We want to help you see that God invites you to draw near. He *wants* you to. Below are some visualization exercises to help you experience and remember this invitation.

PRAY

Take a beat. Quiet Yourself. Unclench your jaw, take some deep breaths, and ask God to help you experience his invitations.
Pray, *"Holy Father, Holy Son, Holy Spirit, help me to know, believe, and trust you want me to draw near to you, as you have drawn near to me."*

IMAGINE THE GARDEN

Picture yourself in a beautiful garden—lush, peaceful, filled with light. This is the place where God first walked with Adam and Eve. Hear God's footsteps and His voice calling, "Where are you?" (Gen. 3:9). You know you just messed up, but instead of hiding, you turn toward God. Imagine going to him as he opens his arms and welcomes you into a loving embrace. Despite your rebellion, God still wants you near.

Pause & Reflect
How does it feel to be invited into the Father's presence regardless of what you've done?

HEAR JESUS' CALL

Now imagine Jesus standing before you, His eyes full of kindness. Hear Him speak the words of Matthew 11:28: *"Come to me, all of you who are weary and burdened, and I will give you rest."* Picture yourself stepping toward Him, laying your burdens down at His feet.

Pause & Reflect
What burdens are you carrying that He is inviting you to release?

SEE THE SPIRIT'S PRESENCE

Imagine a gentle flame resting above you, like the tongues of fire at Pentecost (Acts 2:3–4). This flame represents the Holy Spirit filling you. Feel the Spirit's warmth and filling presence.

Pause and Reflect
Where in your life do you need to be reminded that God took up residence inside of you?

IMAGINE THE FUTURE

Now lift your eyes and imagine the New Creation. A loud voice announces, *"Look, God's dwelling is with humanity, and he will live with them"* (Rev. 21:3). See yourself among the people of God, standing in God's light, fully united with Him forever.

Pause and Reflect

How does knowing your story ends in eternal union with God give you comfort today?

Inhale: *God wants me near.*
Exhale: *I will draw near.*

LECTIO DIVINA

I will bless you as long as I live

"God, you are my God; I eagerly seek you. I thirst for you; my body faints for you in a land that is dry, desolate, and without water.

So I gaze on you in the sanctuary to see your strength and your glory.

My lips will glorify you because your faithful love is better than life. So I will bless you as long as I live; at your name, I will lift up my hands.

You satisfy me as with rich food; my mouth will praise you with joyful lips.

When I think of you as I lie on my bed, I meditate on you during the night watches because you are my helper; I will rejoice in the shadow of your wings. I follow close to you; your right hand holds on to me.

But those who intend to destroy my life will go into the depths of the earth. They will be given over to the power of the sword; they will become a meal for jackals. But the king will rejoice in God; all who swear by him will boast, for the mouths of liars will be shut."

PSALM 63
CSB

READ THE PASSAGE TWICE

WHAT WORD OR PHRASE IS THE LORD HIGHLIGHTING FOR ME?

PAUSE

WHAT INVITATION DO I SENSE THE LORD IS EXTENDING TO ME?

PAUSE

WHAT WOULD IT LOOK LIKE TO SAY "YES" TO THAT INVITATION?

There are over 8 billion people on the planet, and God uniquely wired each one of us. How each of us most naturally and comfortably connects with God is different. And, that's a beautiful thing.

While there is great wisdom in learning to grow in our spiritual disciplines—habits, rhythms, and practices that foster deeper spiritual connection—we want to encourage you to find the paths that most easily connect for you. Make those well-worn paths so that you can be energized to grow in others.

Below are some exercises to help discern which practices you most enjoy and come easiest to you. As you practice, use the checkboxes to notice what you feel, and the scale below to reflect on how your heart responds.

THERE ARE NO RIGHT ANSWERS HERE—ONLY INVITATIONS
TO NOTICE HOW GOD MEETS YOU.

● READING GOD'S WORD
Read Psalm 119:103–105

Ask: *When I engage Scripture, what stirs my heart most?*

- Deeper study, drilling down into a passage and its meaning?
- Meditating on a single verse for my soul?
- Praying Scripture back to God?

NOTICE WHAT YOU FELT

- ☐ CALM
- ☐ CURIOUS
- ☐ WARM
- ☐ PRESENT
- ☐ RESTLESS
- ☐ HEAVY
- ☐ PRESSURED
- ☐ PEACEFUL

HEART RESPONSE

●————————●————————●————————●
DRAINING   NEUTRAL   GROUNDING   LIFE-GIVING

WORSHIPING GOD IN CREATION
Read Psalm 19:1–2

Take a slow walk outside with no phone or distractions.

Ask: *How do I sense God in creation? How does this draw me closer to God?*

NOTICE WHAT YOU FELT

☐ CALM
☐ CURIOUS
☐ WARM
☐ PRESENT
☐ RESTLESS
☐ HEAVY
☐ PRESSURED
☐ PEACEFUL

HEART RESPONSE

DRAINING   NEUTRAL   GROUNDING   LIFE-GIVING

WORSHIP IN ALL VOLUMES
Read Psalm 100 and 131

This week, intentionally engage in two different styles of worship and check in with yourself after.
- Lively, singing and praising God
- Quiet, still meditative worship

Ask: *Which way do I sense God's nearness more naturally?*

NOTICE WHAT YOU FELT

☐ CALM
☐ CURIOUS
☐ WARM
☐ PRESENT
☐ RESTLESS
☐ HEAVY
☐ PRESSURED
☐ PEACEFUL

HEART RESPONSE

DRAINING   NEUTRAL   GROUNDING   LIFE-GIVING

SERVING OTHERS, LOVING NEIGHBORS
Read Matthew 25:35–36

Spend time serving someone in a simple way.
- Encouraging words
- A meal
- Practical help

Ask: *When I serve, do I sense God's presence more deeply?*

NOTICE WHAT YOU FELT

- ☐ CALM
- ☐ CURIOUS
- ☐ WARM
- ☐ PRESENT
- ☐ RESTLESS
- ☐ HEAVY
- ☐ PRESSURED
- ☐ PEACEFUL

HEART RESPONSE

DRAINING   NEUTRAL   GROUNDING   LIFE-GIVING

SILENCE & SOLITUDE PRACTICE
Read 1 Kings 19:11–12

Sit silently for 10 minutes, asking God to meet you in the "gentle whisper."

Ask: Did I connect with God in this stillness? Do I desire more stillness?

NOTICE WHAT YOU FELT

- ☐ CALM
- ☐ CURIOUS
- ☐ WARM
- ☐ PRESENT
- ☐ RESTLESS
- ☐ HEAVY
- ☐ PRESSURED
- ☐ PEACEFUL

HEART RESPONSE

DRAINING   NEUTRAL   GROUNDING   LIFE-GIVING

COMMUNITY VS. SOLITUDE
Read Acts 2:42–47

Try one day of intentional solitude and another of intentional fellowship. Reflect on which environment helps you draw near most naturally.

Ask: Do I feel closer to God in a room full of believers (praying, worshiping, studying) or when I am alone with Him?

NOTICE WHAT YOU FELT

- ☐ CALM
- ☐ CURIOUS
- ☐ WARM
- ☐ PRESENT
- ☐ RESTLESS
- ☐ HEAVY
- ☐ PRESSURED
- ☐ PEACEFUL

HEART RESPONSE

DRAINING   NEUTRAL   GROUNDING   LIFE-GIVING

TALKING TO GOD
Read 1 Thessalonians 5:16-18

Spend some time in extended prayer.

Ask: *Do I feel closer to God as I spend time in prayer?*

NOTICE WHAT YOU FELT

- ☐ CALM
- ☐ CURIOUS
- ☐ WARM
- ☐ PRESENT
- ☐ RESTLESS
- ☐ HEAVY
- ☐ PRESSURED
- ☐ PEACEFUL

HEART RESPONSE

DRAINING   NEUTRAL   GROUNDING   LIFE-GIVING

UNIQUE & UNIQUELY

These are just a few of the many, many ways people can grow in their *union with Christ*. If, after doing these exercises, one of them stirs your desire to draw closer to God, continue practicing, dig deeper, and lean in. While all of them are good and important to cultivate, give yourself permission to pay attention to how your unique wiring uniquely draws you near to God.

Inhale: *God, I want to seek you.*
Exhale: *Help me draw near to you.*

DEVOTIONAL

Luke 10:38-42 CSB

"While they were traveling, he entered a village, and a woman named Martha welcomed him into her home. She had a sister named Mary, who also sat at the Lord's feet and was listening to what he said. But Martha was distracted by her many tasks, and she came up and asked, "Lord, don't you care that my sister has left me to serve alone? So tell her to give me a hand."

The Lord answered her, "Martha, Martha, you are worried and upset about many things, but one thing is necessary. Mary has made the right choice, and it will not be taken away from her.""

Sadly, this story in the Gospel of Luke—featuring two faithful sisters—often gets weaponized against Martha. When that happens, we fail to see the main point of Luke's story: choosing the better thing.

When Jesus enters their home, Martha busies herself with preparations—a very normal practice of hospitality for that day. Martha has done nothing wrong. Mary, on the other hand, chooses to sit at Jesus' feet, listening to the Messiah's teaching.

Martha, who is doing a good thing, grows frustrated with Mary, who in her mind, is failing to uphold the cherished value of hospitality. But, Jesus gently corrects her: *"Martha, Martha, you are worried and upset about many things, **but one thing is necessary.** Mary has made the right choice, and it will not be taken away from her."*

This is a powerful moment in the Scriptures as Jesus shows that the one necessary thing is drawing near to him in devotion and humility. Sitting at a teacher's feet was the position of a disciple—something unusual for women in that culture. But Jesus not only welcomed her presence, but He also defended her choice.

Nearness to Jesus is the better portion, the marrow of life that gives meaning and purpose to our daily tasks.

With Jesus' affirmation of Mary's choice, he teaches us that drawing near to Him in devotion is the greatest priority for every follower.

The "many things" that occupied Martha are not foreign to us today—and they aren't necessarily bad things. Our lives fill quickly with tasks, obligations, and distractions.

But the "one thing necessary" is God's presence. Mary shows us that nearness to Jesus—hearing His voice, receiving His teaching, resting at His feet—is the better portion, the marrow of life that gives meaning and purpose to our daily tasks.

REFLECTION QUESTIONS

WHAT "MANY THINGS" TEND TO DISTRACT YOU FROM SITTING AT JESUS'
FEET?

HOW DO YOU IMAGINE MARY FELT AS JESUS DEFENDED HER CHOICE
TO DRAW NEAR?

WHAT IS ONE SPIRITUAL DISCIPLINE YOU CAN PRACTICE THIS WEEK TO SIT IN
THE PRESENCE OF GOD, DRAWING NEAR?

Looking back at your discernment activities from this week, pick one spiritual discipline to focus on this week.

Take time each day to draw near to God.

Afterwards, take some time to reflect and meditate on the experience.

	How did I feel when I was connecting with God?
□ READING GOD'S WORD	
□ WORSHIPING GOD IN CREATION	
□ WORSHIP IN ALL VOLUMES	
□ SERVING OTHERS, LOVING NEIGHBORS	
□ SILENCE & SOLITUDE	What was pulling me away from God in that moment?
□ COMMUNITY VS SOLITUDE	
□ TALKING TO GOD	

How does spending that time with God help my view of how God feels about me?

Are there any things or steps I need to help me strengthen this practice?
- Calendar?
- Accountability?
- Journal?
- Remove distractions?
- Beliefs that need to be corrected?

At the end of my life, if I connected with God daily like this, what would be true of my relationship with the Lord? Myself? My loved ones?

What is one word I would use to describe this experience?

LECTIO DIVINA

Walk by the Spirit

"I say, then, walk by the Spirit, and you will certainly not carry out the desire of the flesh. For the flesh desires what is against the Spirit, and the Spirit desires what is against the flesh; these are opposed to each other, so that you don't do what you want. But if you are led by the Spirit, you are not under the law.

Now the works of the flesh are obvious: sexual immorality, moral impurity, promiscuity, idolatry, sorcery, hatreds, strife, jealousy, outbursts of anger, selfish ambitions, dissensions, factions, envy, drunkenness, carousing, and anything similar. I am warning you about these things—as I warned you before—that those who practice such things will not inherit the kingdom of God.

But the fruit of the Spirit is love, joy, peace, patience, kindness, goodness, faithfulness, gentleness, and self-control. The law is not against such things. Now those who belong to Christ Jesus have crucified the flesh with its passions and desires. If we live by the Spirit, let us also keep in step with the Spirit."

GALATIANS 5:16-25
CSB

READ THE PASSAGE TWICE

WHAT WORD OR PHRASE IS THE LORD HIGHLIGHTING FOR ME?

PAUSE

WHAT INVITATION DO I SENSE THE LORD IS EXTENDING TO ME?

PAUSE

WHAT WOULD IT LOOK LIKE TO SAY "YES" TO THAT INVITATION?

When we grow deeper in our union with Christ, it tends to overflow into the rest of our lives. We become a non-anxious presence around others, as they experience the fruit of the Spirit in us.

When you accept the Father's invitation to grow closer, spend time practicing your union with Jesus, and allow the Spirit to enliven and strengthen you, you live differently. Those who live life resting in the love of God can then turn around and demonstrate that love to others. Love begets love.

Paul tells us that the evidence of this Spirit-filled union with Christ is healthy fruit of love, joy, peace, patience, kindness, goodness, faithfulness, gentleness, and self-control.

Take some time to ask yourself, when am I most easily demonstrating this fruit:

LOVE

When am I most motivated by selfless care and commitment to others? What helps me to be more loving?

JOY

When is my heart most anchored in God's goodness, even when circumstances are hard?

PEACE

When is it easiest to experience an inner calm because I trust God?

PATIENCE

When am I at my best to respond lovingly when things don't go my way or when others frustrate me?

KINDNESS ——

When is it easiest for my words and actions to reflect God's tenderness toward others?

GOODNESS ——

When am I able to choose what God deems right and life-giving, even when it costs me?

FAITHFULNESS ——

When am I at my most dependable and steady in my commitments to God and others?

GENTLENESS ——

When do I especially handle others with humility and care, especially those who are vulnerable?

SELF-CONTROL ——

When am I most able to resist impulses and follow God's desire for my life?

DRAW NEAR TO GOD AS HE DRAWS NEAR TO YOU

Take a look at your answers to those reflections.
What common threads, moments, situations, etc. do
they have in common? Those commonalities can be
a helpful guide to encourage us to the rhythms,
practices, and habits that lead us to Christ, which in
turn yield more fruit.

The big question: How can you best draw near to
God in a way that the fruit of the Spirit flows out of
your time with the Lord?

Inhale: *Lord, I want to exhibit healthy fruit.*
Exhale: *Help me cultivate a Spirit-led life.*

DEVOTIONAL

Revelation 21:3–4 CSB

"Then I heard a loud voice from the throne: Look, God's dwelling is with humanity, and he will live with them. They will be his people, and God himself will be with them and will be their God. He will wipe away every tear from their eyes. Death will be no more; grief, crying, and pain will be no more, because the previous things have passed away"

Revelation 21 gives us one of the most breathtaking visions in all of Scripture and a picture of where we're headed someday.

What a promise: in the New Heavens and New Earth, God Himself will personally wipe away tears. Every grief will be healed, every sorrow undone, every pain silenced. The brokenness we live with now—the sting of death, the ache of loss, the wounds of injustice—will be no more.

God's final word over creation is not suffering but restoration. All that is broken will be repaired. All that is chaotic will be tamed in peace. All the sad things will be undone.

If God's ultimate plan is to end sorrow and pain, then we are called—through the Spirit's power—to embody that future reality in the present. We become agents of comfort, justice, healing, and peace in this broken world. We become walking, talking, breathing testimonies of God's goodness and desire to make all things new.

As Spirit-filled people, we are invited to begin living now as citizens of the world to come. Every act of kindness, every tear we help dry, every injustice we confront, and every word of hope we speak is a small foretaste of that promised day when God Himself will make all things new.

UNION WITH CHRIST CREATES BEAUTY, GOODNESS, HEALING, PEACE, LOVE, AND JOY FOR US AND FOR THE WORLD.

But this picture of the future actually reaches backwards to us today.

Eschatology determines ethics. Or, in other words, what we believe about the end should impact how we live today. Who we will be then is what we're invited by God to be now. Our hope for tomorrow shapes how we live today.

People who practice their union with Christ can then create thin spaces where others experience heaven and earth reuniting.

REFLECTION QUESTIONS

WHAT SPIRIT-FILLED PRACTICES CAN YOU EMBODY TODAY TO BRING
A GLIMPSE OF THE NEW CREATION INTO THE WORLD—COMFORTING OTHERS,
PURSUING JUSTICE, OR LIVING IN HOPE?

TAKE A MOMENT AND CONSIDER THOSE GOD HAS PLACED IN YOUR LIFE.
HOW CAN YOU ENCOURAGE THEM WITH THIS MESSAGE OF HOPE?

IMAGINE

For our final practice, we are going to spend some time imagining the New Heavens and New Earth as a way to spur us to greater unity now.

PREPARE YOURSELF

Find a quiet place. Take a few deep breaths, unclench your jaw, and relax. Pray: *"Holy Spirit, open my imagination to Your promises. Help me see the world as You are making it."*

PICTURE THE NEW HEAVENS AND NEW EARTH

Close your eyes and imagine the vision of Revelation 21.
See a radiant city, shining with God's glory. Picture streets filled with joy and laughter, not sorrow. Imagine families reunited, neighbors living in harmony, nations gathered without division.

Hear the words echoing: *"He will wipe away every tear from their eyes. Death will be no more; grief, crying, and pain will be no more"* (Rev. 21:4 CSB).

Pause here
What do you notice most vividly?
What fills you with hope?

IMAGINE YOURSELF
IN THAT WORLD

Visualize yourself in this renewed creation. You are
whole—no fear, no guilt, no shame. You are surrounded
by love, belonging, and peace. You see Christ's face,
radiant with kindness, and know you are home.

Pause here

*What do you feel in your body as you imagine this
reality? Relief? Joy? Freedom?*

BRING THEN
TO NOW

Let that vision spill back into your life today.

Ask yourself

If this is my destiny, how might I live differently now?

*If this is the world Christ is bringing, how can I begin
to reflect it in my choices today?*

*If grief and pain will one day end, how can I offer
comfort and healing now?*

DRAW NEAR TO CHRIST

Finally, imagine Jesus beside you—not just in the future vision, but right now. Hear Him say, "Remain in me, and I in you" (John 15:4 CSB).

Let His nearness remind you that union with Him is both the pathway and the power to live toward the New Heavens and New Earth even today.

PRAY

"Lord Jesus, give me eyes to see Your future and strength to live it now. Draw me near, that my life may echo the world You are making."

Inhale: *Lord, I am fully yours.*
Exhale: *Draw me near and grow me in your likeness.*

Union is part of a larger story.

At The Well Summit, we create spaces for those who sit in the
tension of feeling too much and not enough to slow down, engage
Scripture, tend to the inner life, and listen for God's gentle
invitations—together.

Through retreats, gatherings, and discipleship experiences, we
believe healing and formation happen best when we are with God
and with others.

If this study stirred something in you, we'd love to keep walking
together. You're always welcome to
learn more and join us.

THEWELLSUMMIT.COM

amen.